LESSONS

FROM

UNDER A TRACTOR

Karen Kendig

LESSONS
FROM
UNDER A TRACTOR

PAKARADOKIA PRESS

Kiowa, Colorado

Published by *Pakaradokia Press*
P. O. Box 292
Kiowa, Colorado 80117

Library of Congress Cataloging-in-Publication Data

Kendig, Karen.
 Lessons from under a tractor / Karen Kendig.
 p. cm.
 ISBN 0-9640889-0-8

 1. Life.   I. Title.
BD431.K45 1994   814'.54
                                          QBI94-832

Library of Congress Catalog Card Number: 94-92138

Dedicated to my husband,
Jeff...
without whom
there would be no tractor...
no book...
no laughter...
no tears...
and life less abundant!

ACKNOWLEDGEMENTS...

There are multitudes of people who have passed in and out of my life, shaping my beliefs and providing me with a vast array of experiences. I send my gratitude out into the universe for all of you to receive.

A special thank you, from the bottom of my heart, to Jim and Darlene. Your lives together have taught me the true meaning of abundance and plenty.

Dear Reader,

I grew up in the city, graduated from high school, went to college, obtained two advanced degrees in education, got married and bought a home. I felt my life unfolding like a complex mathematical equation, the answer to which I could never find.

Then, in the summer of 1991, my husband and I uprooted our four children from suburbia and transplanted them in rural America. I found the answer I was looking for and my problems were solved.

Within seven months of our move we had purchased a riding lawn mower, three horses, four geese, a four wheel drive pick-up, three thousand dollars worth of barbed wire, twelve rolls of poultry netting, four pygmy goats, a Massey-Ferguson tractor and a partridge in a pear tree!

The purchase of the tractor proved to be the most costly. In the fall of 1993, while attempting to help my son mend fences, I tipped the 2000-pound tractor, pinning my leg beneath its weight.

From that point forward, I have called the mighty tractor Missy. Missy Ferguson. The name sounds innocent enough, but that sweet young thing ate me for lunch!

Missy has taught me more about life than any

installment loan in my credit history! From the moment of impact through physical therapy, the lessons she has taught me have proven to be invaluable.

I believe the lessons Missy has to share will be of value to you also and with a lot less pain!

With eager anticipation,

K.K.
Kiowa, Colorado

TABLE OF CONTENTS

OCTOBER 6, 1993

A tractor fell on me. For ten very long minutes, the leg I use to press the accelerator on my mini-van, kick the cat out of the trash and keep my balance in the shower was pinned beneath a 2000-pound Massey-Ferguson tractor. Thus the term *heavy metal*.

As the tractor fell, the thought that this could not be happening to me occurred simultaneously with the slow motion vision of the massive red beast falling on my leg. Then, it hit my calf with a pressure that is still indescribable.

Within seconds of the impact, I heard myself screaming uncontrollably. Then, with the help of my son, I made a feeble attempt to lift the tractor off my leg. I felt my son turn the steering wheel on the toppled tractor and I heard myself scream at him to stop and go get help.

For the next few moments, all alone, with no where to go and nothing to do, I made a quick assessment of my predicament.

I will not die, Zachary will get help.

I will not have to cut my own leg off with a pocket knife, Zachary will get help.

I may lose my leg...

How long will I be here?

...***When*** will Zachary get help?

Then the pressure on my leg reminded me of child birth and my subconscious took over. Like a Kurt Vonnegut novel, my stream of consciousness led me to the hypnosis I learned in prenatal classes. Without any conscious will, I began to count and breathe, suddenly functioning somewhere between pain and sleep.

Unaware of time or space, my hand was lowered from the tractor horn it had been clutching in desperation. An unfamiliar face came into focus.

"Where are you hurt?" A voice asked.

"My leg." I responded feebly. The voices became jumbled as intense relief overwhelmed me. Help had arrived!

"Karen...Karen!" another voice pleaded.

"Let's see if we can get this thing off of her."

"Somebody get that truck over here. We need the winch."

"Turn the motor off first, before someone else gets hurt." I heard another voice say.

"Just get over here."

"Can we dig her leg out?"

The pressure let up just a little as they dug the sand out from under my trapped leg.

"Can you lift your body so I can get under you?"

"My leg is twisted."

"I know. Lift up so I can get under you to pull you out."

"Hurry! Get that winch on here."

"There's a kink in the chain."

"Get the kink later. Let's get this tractor off her, now."

"If we don't get the kink out, it may break and fall on her again....There."

The body, wedged under my own, pulled at my arm pits and moved me out from under the tractor's grasp.

The pain grew stronger. The counting continued. And the lessons from under a tractor were about to begin...

THE YEAR
OF THE TRACTOR

Have you ever noticed how bad things come in pairs, or maybe even quintuples? The year of the tractor was a good example. Bad luck, karma, misfortune, tough breaks, evil fortunes, ill winds, rainy days, whatever you want to call it, my entire family was experiencing it.

The first of the year started out rather slow. My husband and I didn't pay much attention to the decline in revenues in his business because small businesses always have their ups and downs and the first of the year has traditionally been slow. When we got behind on a couple of payments no one panicked because we had been through this before.

In the spring we were still behind, but there was not time to worry about that because the sheep kept getting out and we had to put up new fence. The dogs got out of their pens and massacred all our chickens and ducks. Their attempts to murder the geese were thwarted, though, by the birds' foul dispositions! After that, many of our weekends were spent building dog runs and houses.

With spring and new birth also comes the death of baby animals and we had more than our share. Lambs and kids died. Puppies were born dead.

During an electrical storm, lightening struck the ground knocking my son off his feet and shorting the electrical systems in the house. Another son had so many cases of strep throat and ear infections that he had to have a third set of tubes inserted into his ears and a tonsillectomy and adenoidectomy performed.

The roller coaster was gaining speed and there seemed to be no end in sight.

The long, hot summer arrived and our van broke down as we were headed out of state to a family reunion. When we returned from our trip, six persons trapped inside a pickup truck for 700 miles, my daughter's horse began to colic for the sixth time in two months. The vet was unable to bring her out of it this time and the horse had to be put down.

Tears flowed. Hopes were shattered and I wondered what more might be in store for us.

In early August, I finally realized that due to new insurance regulations, my husband's income had been permanently decreased by 25 % and our budget would have to be chiseled down as well. By the end of August, my dear grandfather, who was always like a father to me, was diagnosed with liver cancer.

By October, the old saying *things can't get any worse* was proven to be false when the tractor with a diabolical mind of her own, fell on me.

Things looked pretty bleak and the more I sat and thought about them, the worse they looked. I began to drown in my own self-pity. I just sat there and let life keep knocking me down.

I love the ocean. I like listening to the waves hitting the shore and admire the sun and the moon dancing over the water. My encounters with the ocean have been very brief, however, and limited to a few vacations in California and Mexico. I live in Colorado so it's very unlikely you'll ever see me at the beach and the chances are even slimmer that you'll see me in the ocean.

I'm afraid of water. I swim at the hot springs at Glenwood Springs as a courtesy to my family, and I took swimming lessons with my children when they were infants because the lessons are held in the shallow end. But swimming in the ocean is not my idea of fun.

Instead, I stand with my back to the waves and let them push me around. They jump on my back, wrap chains of seaweed around my ankles and spray salt water in my eyes and up my nose. By the time the waves are done chastising me, I've been pushed back to shore and left battered and broken.

The year of the tractor was like that. For awhile I just let the bad times get the best of me, bullying me into a state of depression. I wallowed in self-pity, bathed in my tears and sunk deeper and deeper into what seemed to be a bottomless pit of misfortune. I even resorted to putting my head in my hands and swaying back and forth with mournful sighs coming at eighteen-second intervals. I convinced myself there was no way out and no end in sight.

One morning, after laying in bed tossing and turning, crying and sighing, all of a sudden I sat bolt upright and caught a fresh spray of optimism. Like a surfer riding on top of the waves, I decided to go with the flow.

A little voice inside of me told me to use this time of convalescence to put my life in order, write about my experiences and consider what I truly believe. My husband borrowed money and invested in more education and certification for his career. Our entire family took advantage of the flexibility of home schooling to spend time with my grandfather. As a family, we dug deep into our souls and, using a magnifying glass, tried to find the speck of light in every dark corner.

It was not long before our luck changed. The sun began to shine. And I began to believe good times were just around the corner. It's the same life. The same ocean. Just a different perspective. I decided that I couldn't stay in one place and let the salt water consume me. I had to jump in and ride the waves while the surf was up.

Does the water still frighten me?
To death!
Will I ever go surfing, literally?
I went water skiing once with two life jackets
on and a big life preserver around my waist.
It could happen!

WHAT A MESS!

Life is messy. It took me a long time to realize that. I've known for a long time that life isn't fair. Every parent knows that. It's one of the DNA threads that lies dormant until the carrier becomes a parent and then it just automatically finds its way into every conversation. *"Life isn't fair."*

But I really did believe that life was tidy. I grew up that way. Everything was in its place, neat, uncluttered and dusted. My mother brought me up to live by a daily schedule and a monthly calendar. Events were planned well in advance. NOTHING happened spur of the moment.

I was an only child so the house was also calm, quiet and free from bickering. I kept my room clean and had the bathroom scrubbed by bedtime every Saturday night. For eighteen years we had a big dinner at one o'clock every Sunday and spent the rest of the day at church. My life was orderly... predictable... compulsive. (I am sure my mother orchestrated our lives that way in reaction to the first year of my life when my twenty-three year old father died an agonizing death from lymphoma.)

At the age of nineteen, however, everything changed. I married a man who to this day can only tell time on the hour, give or take fifty-five minutes. He has never had a quiet muscle in his body and filling each day with as many surprises as possible is his nature. For the first five years of our marriage my life began to get cluttered, but it was nothing I couldn't handle. There was always time to pick up, organize and plan ahead. Solitude and cleanliness were still attainable.

After seven years of marriage and two babies, I began to lose control. Trying to keep a tidy life was driving me crazy. The house was always cluttered. The diaper pail reeked. Peace and quiet came at hour intervals throughout the night. The calendar marked the days of the week, but no longer could it assure me that I would actually make it to an engagement. In desperation, I gave up sewing my children's clothes when the dress I finally finished for my daughter was no longer her size.

On our nineteenth wedding anniversary we counted four children (one girl and three boys), twenty acres and over a hundred forms of animal life in our care. I clearly had a big mess on my hands. The only problem was I clung to the notion that life was meant to be tidy. It had worked for my mother. Why not for me?

I couldn't keep the house clean for more than a few hours, even after everyone had pitched in to help. The nose prints of several varieties of dogs and goats, along with muddy hand prints, became permanent window decorations. I became a skilled naturalist, able to identify the type of birds on my

porch by their droppings. The only way I could live
with my guilt was to resort to apologies and excuses.

"Excuse the mess. Our calf has the
scours. No, that's not from the cow.
That's someone's chocolate pudding.
I just didn't have time to clean it up
because the calf has scours!"

"Let me just move these papers so
you can sit down. Oops, sorry about
that. Those marbles can really play
havoc with your hemorrhoids. I'm so
embarrassed by this mess. If the
fence hadn't needed mending, I
would have had this place sparkling."

"Oh, I guess that tomato was on the
skylight the last time you were here.
That was quite a food fight. Jeff's
been so busy he just hasn't had time
to find the ladder."

The excuses were endless and often feeble,
but I found the perfect excuse for all time was
hurting my leg. No one expects you to do anything
when you've been crushed by a tractor. It is
expected that everything will fall to pieces and at

25

various times it did. We had visitors coming and going all the time, dropping in to express their concern and then tripping over something on the way to the bathroom. Everything was a complete mess, but I never once felt like apologizing for it. Let me tell you why.

The day I tipped the tractor was pretty messy. There was blood and dirt and sand all over me. Straw was in my hair and my pony tail was on crooked. The nurse cut my pants to get to the wound and I hadn't bothered to change my underwear when I got up that morning.

When I got home from the clinic, dirty laundry was spread all over the bedroom floor and the flies were having an orgy on the breakfast dishes. As I lifted my head off the couch to shoo a goose off the front porch, I had to peek around peanut butter hand prints to be able to see where he flew. The yard, the house, my body, my life were the embodiment of all that is messy in the world and, for the first time in my life, I embraced the mess and welcomed it into my home.

And to this day, if I can see the mess, I know I'm alive!

CHOCOLATE

You tell me. Which would you rather die from? A falling tractor or brownies? I mean, really!

Before my accident, I was a pretty avid health food nut. The teachers at my school were always entertained by the healthy concoctions I brought for lunch. They were in awe of my magnificent willpower over Friday morning doughnuts and after school candy bars. They couldn't say enough about my petite figure and when my first child was born, one of my co-workers gave me a health food cookbook for babies.

I saw the bodies of my family as temples where I would allow no junk food to enter and desecrate their holy vessels!

When it came to my children, I was the champion of denial.

"No you cannot have a cookie for snack. How about a piece of cheese?"

"Yes I know the other kids are going trick-or-treating. We're going to the haunted house and home for a movie. Doesn't that sound like fun?"

The rules became less rigid by the time our fourth child was born. However, the guilt-inflicting, disgusted tone of my voice became my weapon of deterrence.

"Yes, if you must."

"Only one a day."

"Maybe after dinner, if you're good!"

When my husband would sit in front of the television late at night eating chocolate ice cream and peanuts, I would chastise him for being so weak. In the middle of a chocolate peanut butter bar and a glass of milk, I would remind him of his heart and his responsibilities to his loving family. And each morning began the same.

> *"How about a piece of toast and yogurt instead of the same old peanuts and chocolate milk, dear?"*

And his answer was always the same.

> *"Be sure you put enough chocolate powder in the milk this time. It was a little weak yesterday."*

Then off he went to work, a chocolate mustache on his lips and a quarter pound of shelled nuts in his gut.

Where did all this willpower and denial leave me? On a dark and lonely alley somewhere between Bitter Street and Frustrated Drive, denying myself the hot fudge sundae today because tomorrow I might have high cholesterol...diabetes...heart disease... or worse, cellulose thighs.

Well, Missy changed all that! From the day of the accident, when caring neighbors brought over a plate of brownies, to my mother-in-law who several times brought in elaborate, high fat meals, to my dear friends who drove sixty miles three times to pick me up and take me to Dairy Queen and back home again, I have indulged myself with no thought for tomorrow...and without an ounce of guilt.

TODAY'S MOTTO: BETTER TO DIE FROM CHOCOLATE THAN THE WEIGHT OF A TRACTOR.

OR: WE'RE ALL GOING TO GO SOMETIME. WHY NOT MAKE IT A PLEASANT TRIP?

I know I'm tipping the scales much too far to the right these days, having lived on the other end for so long. And I realize that as soon as I'm not so stressed (desserts spelled backwards), I should really nudge myself back to the center of the scale. Balance. That is what it's all about. Lack of balance knocked Missy off her fifty-six inch wheel base!

I understand the importance of balance. I do. But for now, pass the ice cream. The hot fudge is getting cold!

TIME TRAVEL

I believe in time travel. I didn't before. The idea of visiting another time period simultaneously occurring with my own was unthinkable. Today the concept intrigues me. The actual details escape me, but the general idea is almost in my grasp.

As an elementary school teacher it was always one of my responsibilities to teach time. It was just another mathematical unit of measure to be memorized and used on a daily basis. One minute equals sixty seconds, one hour equals sixty minutes. There are twenty-four hours in a day and three hundred sixty-five days in a year. Time is measurable.

How do you explain time to a kindergartner who asks, "How long before dinner?"

"One hour," I might say.

"How long is one hour?"

"Sixty minutes."

"No, how long?"

"About as long as two cartoons."

"Okay."

For my kindergartner, time now has meaning; like it does for pilots and train engineers, ministers and doctors. Time derives its meaning from schedules and repetition. It's like knowing that it takes so long to get from Colorado to Nebraska by air and just a little less than that to remove an appendix.

It gives me comfort knowing that next year I will be thirty-nine, not fifty-five, and the year after that I will be forty, not sixteen. (Although nineteen was a pretty good year!) I know Sunday comes before Monday and Thursday after Wednesday. They always will. Winter comes after Fall. Tulips bloom in the Spring, then Summer follows. No matter how smart my children grow to be, I will always be older. And although the difference in age between my mother and myself seems insignificant now that I am an adult, she will always be twenty years older than me. As she was when I was born. As she is today. Time is predictable.

Living from day to day with time being measurable, meaningful and predictable is my reality and yours. Until my accident, the reality of time made the idea of time travel unbelievable. However, time now has another quality; one that must be reckoned with; one that throws it for a loop, turns it in a tailspin, warping the concept as we know it. Time is relative.

I lay pinned under Missy for ten minutes. Ten minutes in a nice, hot shower is not the same ten minutes I was breathing and counting under the tractor. It might be the same three hours I was in labor with my son, but it was not even the same ten minutes it takes to watch water boil!

Consider my children's lives after my accident. My two oldest children were responsible for running the house while their father was at work. They home schooled in the morning, made lunch, washed dishes, cleaned house, attended me, watched their little brothers, did their animal chores, made dinner, washed dishes, did homework and went to bed. Ask them if the days were too long and they will answer, "No. There was never enough time in the day to do the things I wanted to do."

Ask my four year old and his answer will be quite different. His job was to hold my hand every morning while my husband cleaned the wound on my leg. He was there every morning without complaining. He also loved to wait on me, bringing me juice and ice packs. He would lay with me on the couch and keep me company watching cartoons. He told me that the days were too long when he was caring for me. He had no time to play with his friends.

Too long. Too short. The same day.

One day I was in a self-pitying mood, moaning and complaining about my misfortune. I commented to my normally very sympathetic husband that I just wanted this whole ordeal to be over. As was our custom whenever we felt life was hard, Jeff brought up the subject of Jim, a high school buddy now living with Lou Gehrig's disease.

Jim lives at home under the constant care of his wife or home care nurses. He is on a ventilator. Food is pumped into his stomach and he communicates through the raising and lowering of his eyebrows or by moving his lips. His health care runs $30,000 a month and the cost would double if the health care system forces his return to a managed facility in order to give him Medicaid coverage.

Jim is a fighter. He is a photographer. A runner. A husband and son. A jokester and good conversationalist. A friend and inspiration. When this ordeal is over for him, it is **all** over.

You do not have to be in an accident to understand the relativity of time. Look at young lovers. Their love is forever, just like my eighty-plus year old grandparents. An hour in church has multiple values depending on whether you are the minister, a parishioner, or a young child who has to go to the bathroom. What about a one hour rock concert and a one hour middle school band concert? Are they the same? Does the cooking of a two minute egg last as long as a two minute scolding? Does four months with a hole in your leg even come close to equalling one week with AIDS?

The moment Missy began to tip over, I viewed the entire event in slow motion. I felt myself hit the ground. I watched the tractor ever so slowly fall toward me.

"This can't be happening to me," I thought. "This only happens in the movies."

Then the tractor hit my leg and time sped up. Can it actually do that? It did. Will I ever go back in time to that day and alter the course of events so that tractor never leaves the ground? I do, every night while I'm sleeping. Will man ever travel in time? I don't know. What time **is** it?

AH,
FOR A BIT OF PRIVACY

We moved to the country to gain some privacy. For two years my husband and I loaded up the kids and spent every weekend previewing homes with a lot of surrounding land. We were convinced that a long commute to work and shopping centers was worth some peace of mind.

Our home in the suburbs had all the modern conveniences within a contemporary framework. The house sat two feet from both neighbors and what lovely people they were. To the east, she wanted to throw rocks at our dog every time he barked. To the west, he wanted a daily schedule for when my children could and couldn't be on the jungle gym.

Community residents had run over our lawn, driven through the neighbor's garage and smashed into several parked cars across the street. The architectural gestapo told us when to put out the trash and how long it could sit on the curb. They mandated house colors and the type of vehicle that could sit in our driveway. We were desperate to escape our internment in suburbia.

The home we finally moved to is everything the other was not. Twelve acres to the east, forty-four to the north, seventy-five to the west and a seldom traveled dirt road to the south. Trash cans can sit out front for days, because sometimes that's how long it takes the sanitation truck to get here. The siding needs to be stained and nobody cares. Privacy abounds.

Or so it seemed. I am now convinced that only a hermit has complete privacy and that's only if all his relatives are dead! In a small town, the anonymity you once had in the city due to sheer numbers, is lost. The teller at the bank knows your name and social security number by heart. She knows how many overdraft statements have been sent to you in the past month and her facial expressions behind the counter pass their judgement upon you. The dog that used to bark in the suburbs, now roams the countryside, and your new neighbor can't be bothered with rocks. He totes a Winchester. In only one year my husband was in two auto accidents. The same teenager hit him both times! When I tipped the tractor, the whole town had heard the story of the Tractor Woman by supper time.

There is glory in fame, but infamy is embarrassing. Some people look at me in awe. They can't believe a little old school teacher was driving a tractor. Having driven it and survived its crushing blow puts me into some kind of club. Friends, family, farmers and ranchers look at me with respect. I have earned my place in the

Survivors of Big Equipment Hall of Fame.

Others, sometimes the very same people, just look at me and shake their heads. "So you're the Tractor Woman? Why'd you ever do such a dang fool thing?" These diehard country natives consider me an outsider; a dang fool city slicker. Wherever I go, I am known. The privacy I worked so hard to achieve did not survive the accident as well as I.

There is one person in town to whom I will always be grateful, a nurse at the clinic. She assisted the team that treated me the day of my accident. She looked into my white face and glassy eyes. She pulled off my shoe and swept up the sand and straw that fell out. She put cool cloths on my forehead and wiped the dirt from my face. For three hours she came in and out of my room, asking what I needed and if I was in pain. I will never forget her care and concern. But that's not why I'm grateful to her.

I came in the next day to have the swelling of my leg measured and my wound repacked. I had washed and combed my hair and put on makeup. My clothes were clean, right down to my underwear. I had a smile on my face and I was coherent. I looked like a million dollars. Okay, only a hundred, but the point is--I looked better! The nurse showed me to the exam room where she took my temperature and blood pressure. "What are you in for today?" she asked.

"I need to have my leg rechecked," I answered, somewhat surprised at her question.

As I pulled up the leg of my sweat pants to reveal the wrappings, she said, "Oh, you're the Tractor Woman. I didn't recognize you."

Thank God for small favors!

DID YOU PUT ON CLEAN UNDERWEAR THIS MORNING?

Nothing is sacred. I learned that when I had kids. The first time I visited the gynecologist was bad enough, but going into the delivery room took all that I held sacred, dear, PRIVATE and spread it apart for every person with a green mask on to see!

The same thing is true when you're in an accident. I knew a woman who was in a terrible car accident. Her automobile was so crushed that the Jaws of Life had to be used. All her clothes, including her bra, had to be cut off of her so she could be freed from the car. Do you thank them for that?

When I was laying on the exam table and the nurse was cutting off my pants to get to the wound, one of the first things I thought was, "Oh my God! I didn't put on clean underwear this morning!"

I wasn't raised that way. My mother always told me to put on clean underwear every morning in case I was in an accident. I never really knew what she meant, but I assumed it was one of those sayings all mothers use to get their children to do the responsible thing--like "eat everything on your plate, because children are starving in Africa."

Having worked at home for the past three years, I learned quickly that you must get up and clean and dress yourself just as if you were going to an office or pretty soon the day is over, your husband is home and you look like you just got out of bed! I shower, dress, comb my hair and put on makeup every morning. It makes me feel better, saves time and embarrassment when people drop by or unexpected things come up. It also makes me take my job as homemaker, teacher and writer more seriously.

On the day the tractor tipped, I took a shortcut. My oldest son wanted me to help him tighten some fence and he wanted to do it in the morning before an impending storm. I had to help in another son's classroom that afternoon and I knew I would get all dirty and sweaty working on the fence, so I didn't bother to take a shower... brush my teeth... comb my hair... put on makeup... or change my underwear!

The doctor and nurses could have cared less. They were professionals, just like my gynecologist. Their main concern was saving my leg and stabilizing my condition. They did their jobs while I lay on the examination table thinking about my dirty underwear; wondering if they were going to know my secret, along with every other private part of me.

They never knew. The tractor didn't fall on my pelvis, just my calf. And to tell the truth, clean underwear may not matter anyway. My guess is, if the accident is any worse than mine was, your clean underwear won't be clean by the time the doctor gets to you anyway!

LET'S SEE SOME CREATIVITY HERE

I was hurt. My ego was nearly as bruised as my leg. My doctor, who is also a friend and has visited my home on several occasions, told me I wasn't very creative.

I pride myself in being creative. I admire that quality in others and am constantly nurturing it in my own life. My home is filled with my creations. I work at being a creative teacher and I dabble in creative cooking. If she had told me I wasn't very smart, I could have lived with that. But when she said I wasn't creative, it caused me to take a close, hard look at myself.

Her remark was meant as a joke in reply to my flippant statement that having a tractor fall on your leg was a good form of birth control. She responded to my remark by saying that if my leg was keeping us from having sex, I was not very creative.

She has forgotten the remark, I'm sure. I have not.

Her words hit their mark. They made me take a look at my life and my responses to it. I found that my creativity was very selective. I am creative in crafts, writing, storytelling and music. I have a flare for the dramatic and I create fanciful parties. As a teacher and a thinker I pride myself in

45

being creative, but in day-to-day responsibilities, creativity is sorely lacking.

The first unoriginal act I noticed was in the way I disciplined my younger boys. I was current on all the latest ways to manage behavior and had probably tried them all; but when all else failed, I fell back on the ever-effective physical punishment.

> *"Go to your room."*
> *"No."*
> *"Go to your room!"*
> *"No."*
> *"Now!"*
> *"No."*

At this point I normally would have resorted to a spanking on the bottom, but since I was unable to balance without my crutches it was impossible to get into a struggle that I was not equipped to win. So I had to get creative.

> *"If you don't go immediately you'll lose dessert."*

> *"I'm not going."*

> *"You're going to lose television too."*

"Who cares."

"Go to bed now, without any dinner."

"No, Mommy, please. I'll stop."

"It's too late. You should have stopped when I first asked you."

"Please, Mommy, no."

"Go."

"What's for dinner?"

"Leftovers."

"Okay, I'll go, but could I have a peanut butter sandwich first?"

"No!"

This may not seem too creative to you, but not resorting to physical punishment seemed very creative to me. I'll have to tell the doctor.

My doctor's remark made me realize that there are a lot of situations in my life that could use a splash of creativity. Maybe I need to be more creative with my routine. Instead of griping at my children to always mind their manners at the table, maybe we could have a barbarian night when no one eats politely. Then we could have a society night when everyone dresses up for dinner and has to eat a seven course meal by candlelight without the television. Then, once a month at least, I'll know they really know how to behave before royalty.

Maybe I could hide things in the kitchen and the person who does the best cleaning job finds it and wins a prize. We could keep a graph of the time it takes for each person to fold the laundry and the one who does it the fastest doesn't have to do it the next week. The only time I let them listen to the radio full blast could be when they're dusting.

Now you're probably thinking what I thought, "Should children be brought up to believe that everything they'll do in life is fun?" Well maybe not fun, but can I train myself and my children to look at the mundane, creatively? I'm going to give it a try, right after I find that slinky, black negligee my husband bought me last Christmas.

My doctor says I'm not very creative? I'll show her!

THIS IS A TEST

Did you ever think that life is a test? If you pass you move on to another course, or even take an advanced placement; but, if you don't pass, you'll get put in the dummy class, taking it over and over again until you finally get it right. I think about it a lot. It's the only possible explanation I can come up with for all the unexplainable events that occur in our lives.

Examples abound. Why do some really evil people have millions of dollars to throw away on drugs and I can't scrape together the electric payment? Why are all four of my children healthy and my friend's family lost two babies to SIDS? Why did my father die of cancer at twenty-three and my eighty year old grandfather has cancer now?

Do you ever question why young children are sentenced to a life of starvation and disease while others are literally spoiled to death? How does one family member grow up to be a doctor and another a mass murderer? These questions and hundreds more have baffled me forever, causing me to question my own belief system.

A whole new set of questions entered my mind after the initial shock of my accident wore off. Why did I even get on that stupid tractor? Why did it have to fall on my leg? Why didn't it break any bones? Why do I still have my leg when others have lost their lives in similar accidents? What will the next test be like?

I do not understand why some people I know have all the luck, I have a little and others have none. I want to know why this tractor fell on my leg at a time when we needed me to go back to work. And I want to know why my friend, Jim, has to suffer from Lou Gehrig's disease, losing his insurance at a time when he so desperately needs it.

I believe Jim and I both passed our tests this time around. But what I don't understand is why his test continues to be so much more comprehensive than mine. The only explanation I can give relates to prior knowledge. Jim and I come from different backgrounds, different genetics, maybe different lifetimes. The lessons he needs to learn this time around are very different from mine. Although we may both pass all our tests with flying colors, the diplomas we leave with will be very different, preparing us for our next lives ahead.

So what does all this mean when we're in the middle of a personal disaster? Study hard. Learn your lessons well. Be diligent and devout in the education called life so you will get the best grade you possibly can. If you don't, the next test could be a bitch.

Any questions? Good. You may begin.

WHO DO YOU
WANT TO BE
WHEN YOU GROW UP?

During one of my routine checkups, the doctor told me a well kept secret. "On the day of your accident," she said, "one of the nurses told me she wants to be like you when she grows up."

I was shocked... stunned... and actually quite honored, even though we are the same age. As I left the doctor's office, I tried to imagine to which of my numerous qualities she was referring.

My physical appearance? My dirty unkempt hair? My pale, ghostly complexion, a result of shock and fatigue, not to mention I had not put on any makeup that morning. It must have been my impeccable taste in clothing: unironed, 100% cotton shirt and matching beige canvas pants with a broken drawstring waist and a half mast zipper. It could also have been my one irregular Nike running shoe filled with sand and my bare toes with matching elasticized bandage. No I guess not.

Maybe it was my great sense of humor.

"May I cut your pants, Karen?"

"No, not my best pants!"

51

"Can you get your pants off so I can give you a shot to relieve the pain?"

"Just cut 'em off!"

"Roll over and I'll just pull your pants down. You should just feel a little prick!"

"This must be the reason my Mom always told me to wear clean underwear."

"Can you feel this, Karen?"

"..."

"Karen?"

"..."

"Are you still with us?"

"Were you talking to me? If you want a response, tap my shoulder would ya?"

There was no way from our conversation that

day or by her knowing the cause of my injury that she could have longed to have my intelligence. She had no way of knowing I had any.

Maybe she assumed I was a wonderful mother, because my children were so concerned about their saintly mother that they kept a vigil in the waiting room. No, I'm sure she heard them hooting and laughing as they sat in the normally quiet waiting room, swapping jokes with the man who pulled me out from under the tractor! In fact, I think she's the one who asked them to leave and come back in an hour or two!

I racked my brain. Why in the world would she want to be like me?

"You were so stoic," the doctor said.

That took me completely by surprise. Stoic? I was under self-hypnosis, almost unconscious, completely out of character! It didn't seem fair to take credit for something that I didn't consciously do. She shouldn't want to be someone I'm really not.

Since that day, I've had a lot of time to reconsider my position. Maybe we find out who we really are in the midst of a trauma. I am proud of the way I handled myself that day. I'm honored that the nurse wants to be like me when she grows up. I want to be like me when I grow up, too. But there's more to it than that.

People face trauma in their lives everyday. Some of them we hear about on the news and they reveal who they are to the whole world right in the midst of their trauma. We learn about others, long after the fact, as they're forced to testify before a judge of the abuse and assault they have survived; or a cold, boldly printed foreclosure notice in a window may be all that is left of a stoic family.

Some traumas seem so insignificant to the public eye that we tend to overlook the toll they take on our lives. Children lose races and are ignored by their peers. Hateful words are spoken in homes and office buildings. Loved ones pass in and out of our lives, as does our hard earned money. Hardship and disappointment abound. Illness, disease, injuries and mental illness knock at every door. In every home in every land, people are facing their traumas in the dark corners of their souls.

Everyone must perform acts of bravery each day of their life. They may not be newsworthy, but they make us worthy.

Stand up.... Yes, I mean you. Before you read any further, I want you to stand up. Get out of bed and stand tall. If you're with somebody else and you're too embarrassed to get up, excuse yourself and go into the bathroom and lock the door. Or if you're sitting among a crowd of strangers, then put

54

the book down until you can have some privacy.

Are you standing? Shoulders back? Head
held high? Now look straight ahead and imagine me
standing in the room with you, face to face. What
do I look like? It doesn't matter. This is coming
straight from my heart.

I want to be like you when I grow up!

FAMILY MATTERS

Actually, I am very thankful the Massey-Ferguson decided to roll on top of me that morning in October. If it had not, there are some important insights into my family that I would have missed.

One thing I found out is that my youngest son is not the greedy glutton I thought he was. Whenever he sits in front of the television set, my five year old watches all of the commercials and chooses all of the toys he wants to receive for Christmas. He actually says out loud, with a mouthful of pretzels and a super-hero blanket wrapped around him, "Santa, I want that, please." You can hear him any time of the day asking the jolly old soul to give him every piece of junk commercialism has to offer.

This little mogul celebrated his fifth birthday during my convalescence. His father and brothers were out of town. His sister was busy with her horse and I was laying on the couch. We had gone out to dinner the night before to a Mexican restaurant of his choice, but there were no presents, no party, not even a cake. He was spending his birthday, not like a kid, but like an adult.

For most of the day we wrapped ourselves together in his blanket and watched all his favorite videos. Sometimes he would go off by himself to play and I would call him into my room where I was resting to sing Happy Birthday to him. We read books and sang The Old Woman Who Swallowed a Fly (I don't know why she swallowed a fly!). He celebrated this very important fifth birthday with no presents... no cake... no tears... and a smile on his face when he went to bed. I would not be able to cherish that day in my heart if I had been mobile.

Another thing I learned is that my oldest son is an excellent cook. We had some really good meals while I was incapacitated, because other people cooked them. My mother-in-law made a pot roast and we had hash and hot beef sandwiches thereafter. A friend from church made stew, which we ate for several meals. When my grandmother cooked a ham, it only made sense that pea soup should be made from the meat that remained on the bone.

My family is not crazy about legumes, but it is a ritual that when you have ham, some sort of bean dish follows. It was my son's turn to fix the meal. He had a choice of two pea soup recipes and chose the Danish version served with a dollop of sour cream and horseradish sauce. With the pride and hopeful anticipation of every great chef, he chopped and diced, boiled and stirred his half-gallon pan of soup.

Having been taught the extreme importance of cornbread with a bean or lentil dish, my son made a large pan of cornbread with blackberries. It was a gourmet meal set before children who eat hot dogs as their meal of choice! The twelve year old chef and his thirty-eight year old mom were the only ones who actually finished their bowls of soup. (I should confess that I ate several bowls of soup in the weeks that followed until my gag reflex caused me to dump the rest down the drain.) Everyone had seconds on the cornbread and the sour cream and horseradish sauce tasted pretty good over burritos.

To say the least, my son was disappointed. He had worked very hard on a meal that no one appreciated or even liked, not even himself. I tried to praise him for his efforts and show him how much I liked it by eating so many bowls. The grumblings of his siblings and their untouched bowls of soup spoke louder than my words.

Had I been able to make dinner that night, the same thing would have happened. The children would have left the table hungry and I would have been stuck with eating nearly a half-gallon of soup myself. What happened instead was that my oldest son came to understand my frustration at cooking meals and hearing only moans and groans in return. I have also decided that no one should have to eat bean soup or any of its variations. I'll just throw the ham bone to the dogs from now on.

The final insight came from my husband. I

was made to realize that when my husband says he can do everything, he's absolutely right! During the five weeks I was off of my feet, he had to do his job and mine, plus run me around to doctor appointments, clean my wound each day and hold me up in the shower. (He said he didn't mind that part!)

What he learned was that the washer and dryer run all day. The car is rarely in park. Children do not automatically pick up after themselves, even after you tell them to and give them an extra chore because they didn't. Man cannot live off of Ramen noodles alone and dinner doesn't cook itself. He now knows why I am so tired at the end of the day, even though I don't work outside of the home. He understands why checks bounce and who is bouncing them. I believe he comprehends why I rarely wash windows, seldom dust, always make the boys put the toilet seat down and never clean the oven.

If I had not been hurt and unable to do what it is my family thinks I don't do all day, my husband would never have known why it is no one wants to do what I don't do all day. And I would never have known that he really can do everything. Just not very well!

THE HOLY ORDER
OF THE CONFINED

Doing nothing for weeks. That is a teaching technique used by mothers, bums and gurus, all learned philosophers. Observe.

Where mothers are concerned, example may not always be the best teacher. I cook and clean, sew and wash, listen and direct, organize and serve all day long. In return, my husband and children complain about the leftovers, wonder why their favorite shirt with the gum in the pocket has a stain on the pocket and can't find a thing in their rooms aside from a glass of sour milk and a couple dozen candy wrappers.

I believe, from experience, that the best example a mother can provide is to do nothing. When mom is gone or incapacitated for a week or more, strange things begin to happen. If every mother chose the same week to do nothing, the whole world would fall apart.

Entire nations would be buried under household debris, piles of dirty dishes and volumes of bills and school notes. All trade and commerce would stop. Gasoline pumps would stand naked and rusting from a lack of car pools and taxi services to dances, lessons, parties, games, scout meetings and last minute runs to the store. Men and children would starve to death shortly after all the frozen dinners and hot dogs were merely a bad odor passed in the night.

Who would stop the battles over the bathroom and give aid to the poor wretches who can't find enough pocket change for the movies? Who would guard the cradle, protecting the small and weak from monsters and diaper rash?

The philosophy of the first Great Master of Do Nothing Mothers is simple and to the point:

> *Let a mother sit and do nothing for a week and she will have taught her family how to appreciate... a warm meal... a crisp shirt... and boundless hugs.*

The philosophy of bums is more subtle. At first glance, they provide subject material for mini-lectures on what not to become.

> *"Don't drop out of school or that's what you'll have to look forward to."*

> *"If you don't work harder, you could end up like that!"*

> *"Don't ever let me see you begging*

for food. Stand on your own two
feet. "

But on closer examination, something
mystical occurs. Sitting for weeks, unable to work
to pay the bills, hoping the peanut butter didn't run
out before another check came and envisioning
Christmas without a tree or presents, I realized that
the repulsive life-style I so desperately wanted my
children to reject, had a face. Possibly my own. At
that moment, the philosophy of bums took a free
ride on my emotions.

> *How tall might I stand in his worn*
> *out shoes? How blue would my blood*
> *flow beneath his skin? How deep*
> *would the love for my family be,*
> *sitting at his empty table? What kind*
> *of model would I be for my children if*
> *I stood begging for a blanket to cover*
> *their chilled bones?*

Having answered the questions posed by the
second Great Master of Do Nothing, I realized that
sometimes doing nothing is the best any of us can
do. That gave me a bulging pocketful of humility.

I was rather shocked to realize that as
mother, off my feet and unable to be my family's

beck and call girl, I could still have a profound impact on their spiritual growth. I expected such from gurus who sit for weeks meditating and fasting, pondering the meaning of life and philosophizing alone or with other masters. But, unable to sit or fast through more than one meal, mothers rarely receive that kind of respect. The lesson I learned from these holy men who emulate calmness, solitude, introspection, peace, tranquility... everything our busy lives are missing... was quite the opposite of what I expected.

I do not believe the third Great Master of Do Nothing teaches us to get up off our butts and start serving again! His message is quite the opposite. Take time for yourself. Give yourself the love and care you need. Heal yourself and others will be healed. Fasting from self-worth can be hazardous to your health. Don't skimp. When I dish it up in big helpings, my entire family is full.

After being double parked on the living room couch for four weeks, I came face to face with each of these three Great Masters. I wrestled with their lessons in the dark recesses of my soul and I emerged with a new sect, The Holy Order of the Confined.

I still believe in the philosophies of the Great Masters, with the addition of one small detail. A little "do nothing" goes a long way. It can give you bed sores and a stiff neck. Your extremities can fall asleep and your muscles lose their tone. Doing nothing can even cause your motivation to shrivel up and blow away.

The Holy Order of the Confined consists of millions of people confined to wheelchairs and couches, beds and hospital rooms. Some for weeks. Others for a lifetime. We are an anonymous sect who believe the lessons of the Do Nothing Masters are important. Very important. But we don't want to take advantage of our situation, nor it take advantage of us. Our philosophy pushes us off the couch, or at least out of the bean bag chair of self-pity.

That philosophy? *CELEBRATE...* with every muscle that's still working!

A ROSE BY
ANY OTHER NAME...

Juliet Capulet knew nothing about being politically correct. She was a hopeless romantic who made the mistake of falling in love with a boy who was politically unacceptable to her family. But Juliet didn't care. She went so far as to tell Romeo that what he was called meant nothing to her. Juliet loved and adored her Romeo and therefore had the right to say, "That which we call a rose by any other name would smell as sweet."

I have always agreed with Juliet. I guess maybe I've always been a bit of a romantic at heart. I have chuckled to myself many times when "Negroes" wanted to be called "Blacks" and then "African-Americans," or the "retarded" became known as "mentally handicapped" and then "mentally disabled" and now "mentally challenged." I thought it was childish for women to protest being referred to as "doll" or "babe" and for presidents and their wives to have to apologize for not liking certain vegetables. The whole thing seemed silly.

We are who we are no matter what we're called. Right? Take for instance a set of crutches.

I was forced to rely on a pair of crutches for a month. I had used them once before, back in college when I fell off a horse. I remembered them as nothing more than a prop. A resting place. A cradle for my helpless body. Those two metal supports with rubber on both ends allowed me to get back and forth to the bathroom by myself, but otherwise I saw no redeeming qualities in them. They were dangerous on ice and in the shower. They rubbed my armpits raw and made the palms of my hands ache. As far as I was concerned, a crutch by any other name was still a demeaning piece of equipment used by a less than physically competent individual.

Not true!

Ask any of my children. Ask anyone's child, for that matter, who is around an unused pair of crutches. My four year old had never seen a pair before his father brought them home to me. He did not know what they were called and named them himself after watching his previously immobile mother put them to use.

Walking sticks! The name literally makes you want to get up and dance! Walking sticks were not put on this earth solely to provide mobility to the lame. That would be a crutch and a waste of a perfectly fantastic invention. No, walking sticks have as many uses as can be conjured up in the imagination.

My oldest son liked to race down stairs with them, testing his agility and speed against the clock. The two younger boys had sword fights with them and every once in a while shot pretend bullets out the ends. My husband liked to use them to block doors and hallways, making each child promise to be good or give a secret password before they could cross the threshold. I am afraid my daughter is too much like her mother to have found any other uses for the crutches. But, by the time I returned them to the pharmacy, I was proud to admit that I had used them to trip a few kids, tap a few bottoms and throw dirty clothes across the room!

Juliet had a good point. Now that I have experienced walking sticks, I will never again think of them as crutches. I will always remember the pleasure they brought everyone in my family. In fact, more often than not, I couldn't find the suckers when I needed them, because someone else was using them for something other than their intended use.

William Shakespeare was not a hopeless romantic, even though some of his characters were. Shakespeare was streetwise and even though he never heard the term "politically correct," he knew what it meant. He knew that Juliet's words of love were just that, words spoken without a trace of hatred or prejudice. Words spoken out of deep respect and admiration for a person Juliet knew and loved.

If everyone treated others with the respect and admiration Romeo bestowed on fair Juliet, and vice versa, a rose by any other name **would** smell as sweet. But the truth is, we do not live in a small village where everyone knows everyone else (and that made no difference to the Capulets and Montagues anyway). We live in a world where the media gives us a rapid glance at the world and then pushes us to make snap judgements about people we have never met and will never know.

In that kind of world, crutches remain crutches, a spade is a spade (or a nigger) and dolls and babes are sexually harassed in the work place. Shakespeare knew about being politically correct. His young lovers died tragically because the rest of the village, even their own parents, could not see beyond their names to look at the true beauty of the rose.

I don't chuckle much anymore when I hear a new politically correct term. I didn't find it all that outrageous when my high school elected to change their "Redskins" mascot, after Native American students filed a civil suit against the school. I did find it a bit ridiculous that Hillary Clinton had to publicly apologize for not liking peas, but....

Until human beings of all races, creeds,

religions and sexes throw away their crutches and look at the hidden qualities in each individual, we need politically correct terminology. It forces us to exchange our crutches for walking sticks and hopefully gives us a chance to get out there and dance with one another before the whole world is crippled!

JUST BEYOND
MY GRASP

Do you ever get the feeling that the things you want most in life are just beyond your reach? Have you ever wished for someone to just grab it for you and then you could take it from there? If someone else would just do the dirty work for you, you would never need another person's help again.

I believed that. I thought that if I could win the lotto just once, I would never need money again. If a publishing company would accept just one of my books for publication, my confidence would never be shattered again. I had a chance to test the theory while I was off my feet after the accident.

Using my crutches was such an effort that I was constantly asking my children and husband to bring me things. For the first two weeks everyone jumped at my commands and rarely complained. They brought me tea and tissues, books, paper, pillows, and blankets. They turned up the radio and lowered the volume on the television. They answered the phone, helped me into the shower, made me cookies and brewed tea. Everyone seemed to be fine with the arrangement. I know I was! All I had to do was ask and it was given to me.

Then one morning as my husband was rushing around to get to work, I asked him to bring me my sweat pants. He was trimming his beard and did not jump at my request. I was unable to get on with my daily schedule without my pants so I asked him again.

"You can get up and get them yourself," he snapped. "Besides, they're right there beside you on the couch!"

My feelings were hurt and I was embarrassed by my behavior. "Is it really that bad?" I asked.

"You're getting pretty demanding," was his reply. "Let's see if we can't arrange things to make it easier on all of us."

So it began. A table on wheels was placed in the living room with all my writing supplies on it. Books, bills and tea cups also rested there. Towels and wash clothes were moved from the linen closet to the drawers under the sink and a chair sat in the bathtub for quick and easy access to the nearby vanity.

I made a new rule for myself. If I can get it myself I will. It was a royal pain to get around the house on crutches. Everyone else could get it in half the time it took me. But that wasn't the point. It was my life, and if what I wanted was worth having, I needed to find a way to get it myself.

Everything I wanted was just out of my reach. I forced myself to improvise. It was easiest to crawl from the couch to the phone. Picking up laundry and tossing it in the clothes basket was best done off the end of a crutch. To call my children from the barn into the house, I used a whistle. In the shower, I leaned against the cold tile and balanced on one leg. I could carry books and newspapers under my arms along with my crutches, but hot tea and plates of food had to be carried by someone else.

It wasn't long before I realized I was not as limited as I had thought. I also came to realize that nothing was really beyond my grasp. It might take me longer than most. I might be tired and sweaty by the time I arrived at my destination, but I did arrive. Usually no one was around to applaud or praise my accomplishments, but that didn't matter. The credit was all mine and no one could ask for more!

TENNIS ANYONE?

Life is like one of those tennis ball machines. You know the kind. It shoots balls at you to test your skill and stamina. Life is one of those machines gone bad. There is no off switch and if you pull the plug, it just keeps spitting out balls faster than ever.

Just like a tennis game, in life you have no control over what comes over the net at you. The only control you have is in the response.

On a good day, I bat those balls back and forth in a frenzy of excitement, enthusiasm and exhaustion. I am up for the challenge and I feel like a winner. But not even a Wimbleton champion can play the game forever without a breather, and sometimes it seems as if life does not know when to stop serving!

So, at various times in my life, I've had to move to the sidelines, out of harm's way, watching life zing by me. When I have chosen not to respond to the ball, several things have happened. Balls piled up in the corner of the court. Sometimes someone else entered my court, returning the serve that was meant for me. At other times, a stray ball found its way to the outer bounds and whacked me in the head!

By the way, stray balls do not travel alone. They come in cases: twenty cans to a case, a variety of colors available. When those neon balls start bombarding me in the head, I am forced to make a move.

I have considered throwing down my racket and walking off the court forever. But that seems rather permanent, with no guarantee that I will be able to view the court from a box seat up above. Another option would be to crawl in front of the net and lie down on the court in a fetal position with my hands over my head. That way I could shield myself from those fast and powerful balls. However, I'm afraid that eventually a couple ball boys would be sent in to drag my bruised and bloodied body off the court; frozen in fetal defeat. To date, the only viable option I've thought of, when I'm forced to make a move by those relentless balls, is to jump back into the game. But even with both sneakers planted firmly on the court, some of the balls still hit me in the head. Others strike me in the back as I've bent to pick up a dead ball and fling it back at the machine. If I'm quick, I've been able to dodge quite a few or hit some out of bounds. With a little practice and lots of encouragement from the sidelines, I've always gone back to being a skilled player, facing my opponent for the duration.

This time, right in the middle of the game, that crazy machine shot a bowling ball at me, with quite a curve. Injured and feeling defeated, I sat on the sidelines watching the balls dart past me. My whole family was in there swinging at and dodging balls. Some days my husband played with a racket in both hands. Some days neighbors and friends stepped in and racked up a few points, but the balls never stopped coming. And sometimes my position on the sidelines was still within pummelling distance of several stray balls. There was no place to hide. All I could do was watch and learn. Practice from the waist up. Get ready for my comeback.

I'm back in the game now, stronger than before. All the credit goes to one thing, determination. The determination to come back swinging, to face my challenger and return the serve, to perfect my game and have a powerful back hand. Determination is everything. Oh, and love too.

HORROR STORIES

Why do we like horror stories so much? Why do we like to be scared half out of our wits by the tales of ugly, gruesome people and events? Why do we slow down when we approach an ambulance and strain our necks to get a view of its occupants?

When I was growing up, our next door neighbors were ambulance chasers. Every time they heard a siren, they piled the family in the car and took off to find the accident or fire. Why would anyone want to witness someone else's misfortune? I always thought it was a bit demented. It showed signs of immaturity and a lack of compassion and respect for privacy. It wasn't until my accident that I got a handle on the real reason people seek out doom and gloom.

Horror stories abounded when I was injured. They occurred in two forms. Those I told myself, with a flare for the dramatic, to entertain and shock my visitors and phone callers. The others were those told to me by my well-wishers. Why did we share these ghastly tales?

I told my story over and over again, with much attention to gory details, to elicit respect and sympathy.

"I can't believe she laid there for all that time underneath that heavy

tractor. How could she endure such
pain? What a trooper."

"Did you see that terrible hole in her
leg? The tractor just split it open on
impact. It's a wonder her whole leg
wasn't crushed from the force. Poor
thing."

"Her husband has to clean that
wound everyday. She says he sprays
cold salt water into the open wound
and then packs the hole with sterile
gauze, using surgical tweezers! What
an ordeal!"

The truth is, all my stories were true. The
truth is, as I lived through the events and look back
on them, they don't seem so bad. But I kept telling
them with much embellishment anyway. Why do
you think that is?

I think I told my horror story over and over
again to justify my lack of participation in life. It
was also confirmation that I was still alive. The
werewolf doesn't devour everyone he nips. Dracula
doesn't successfully suck all of his victims dry. And
the boogie man is not more powerful than a winch!

But why did everyone who heard my story
feel compelled to tell one just a little more

gruesome? Was it a contest of storyteller's one-up-
manship? Did they want to minimize my pain? I
don't think so. These were very caring and
concerned people I'm talking about, yet they told the
most shuddering tales.

> *"I knew a guy who dumped a tractor*
> *like that and he's paralyzed from the*
> *waist down."*

> *"My uncle lost his arm, up to the*
> *elbow, on a piece of farm equipment.*
> *You know don't you that farms and*
> *ranches have the highest mortality*
> *rate of any occupation due to all that*
> *machinery they use?"*

> *"You should never have let them*
> *move that tractor without a*
> *paramedic there first. I've seen them*
> *lift a tractor off a person's leg and*
> *that was the only thing applying*
> *pressure to a major artery and the*
> *person bled to death! If that ever*
> *happens again, call 911 first. Even if*
> *it takes longer than the neighbor*
> *would, wait for the rescue unit."*

It was their way of saying, "It could be

worse. Thank God you're alive. You're a lucky woman. You need to be more careful."

Isn't that why people chase ambulances or choose horror in various mediums for their entertainment? We gawk at an accident and watch the blood and gore on the nightly news. There is a plethora of rescue and eyewitness shows on television. We go to the movies, rent videos and read frightening accounts of monsters and scum of the earth that make our hair stand up on the back of our necks and send chills up and down our spines. We bite our nails and turn our knuckles blue. We scream and pee our pants, but we always come back for more. Why?

Because horror reinforces the fact that we are so much better off than that poor, helpless victim on the road, on the pages of a book or on the movie screen. Horror stories help to put our everyday fears into perspective. They make us feel lucky.

I must admit, though, I've never been a fan of the macabre. I've never followed the fire truck to a fire and I can't say that I've ever seen an authentic horror movie or taken the time to read anything that might keep me awake at night. Personally, I find my own life to be frightening enough!

IDLE HANDS

I was raised to believe that idle hands are the work of the devil. No one ever actually said that to me, but that's what I thought my mom was conveying to me through her actions. Every minute of every day she was busy doing something. She worked all day, came home, made dinner, did the dishes and then sat down to watch television with a dress to hem or crocheting in her hands. We cleaned, baked and sewed on Saturdays. On Sundays we were at church most of the time, with an occasional drive to the country. Busy, busy, busy.

My grandparents were the first to set the record straight about the value of idleness. I had lots of tea parties with my grandmother and she was always very willing to play hide the button or Tiddly Winks. Grandpa always watched me on Wednesday nights when Mom and Grandma were at choir practice. For two hours I would sit on his lap watching television (Mitch Miller as I recall) and eating popcorn. Now that's idle.

When I was first married, my husband liked to spend Saturday mornings watching the Three Stooges. Watching television on Saturday when we could be painting, or laying sod, or grocery shopping, or entertaining guests was simply a waste of time. Watching the Three Stooges on Saturday when we could be building a chimney, chopping firewood, or storing up nuts for the winter was a sin. Too much idleness causes you to make NYuck, NYuck sounds and poke people in the eyes! When my children were babies I had to work outside of the home for several years, so there was very little idle time. We did lots of fun things on the weekends. We went to shows and parties and museums and such, but very little time was spent on lazy-do-nothing-idleness, except when they would lay in bed with us pretending to sleep or crawling under the covers to play hide and seek. Breast feeding was the closest I got to idle time. I loved it, but I'm not sure it counts.

Now that my kids are older, the only idle time I have is in the car, running them from place to place, and that's not really idle, just wasted!

For nearly five weeks after the tractor fell on me, all I could do was be idle. For the first week I was so doped up on pain medication that I slept most of the time. That doesn't count either. To be idle you must be conscious and let time pass without working. Or, and I like this definition, to consume fuel without being connected with moving parts! That was me.

I read a little and watched a lot of cartoons and videos. Because of my idleness, my youngest son now knows the words to many of the most popular musicals on video cassette. I saw every sunset out my living room window for thirty-five days and ate chocolate covered Bing cherries on the couch. I grew very fond of my idleness. It didn't count, though. Not really. It was forced idleness and not by choice.

It was great because I did not have to feel guilty about being idle. I couldn't do anything anyway. Now, I miss my idleness. I've gone right back to grading papers or folding clothes while I watch television. I don't seem to have a lot of time to snuggle up and watch cartoons with my son. And someone's eaten the rest of the chocolate covered Bing cherries. It is still very hard for me to choose to be idle, but I no longer believe it to be the work of the devil.

Idleness is not unproductive. It just depends on what you're trying to produce. If it's fond memories you're looking for, nothing works better than idleness. I mean it you knucklehead! NYuck, NYuck!

PLAY THAT SONG
BACKWARDS

My physical therapist was the young, athletic type. My guess was he'd never needed his own services and he didn't like country music. The first day I went to see him I was ready to go through my whole sad story once again, just for him. Most everyone I knew had heard it by then and the tellings were fewer and farther between.

He escorted me into a room and had me pull up my husband's sweat pants. (I didn't have a pair of my own and his were so big they never touched the wound as I pulled them up above my knee.) He undressed the wound and asked the predictable question, "What happened?"

"A tractor fell on my leg," I said, ready for the surprised expression and the concerned request for all the gruesome details.

"Don't you know you're not supposed to do that?"

That was it? He didn't ask for a play-by-play description of the accident. He didn't even express concern. He just put my leg into a hot whirlpool. At least he asked if the temperature was okay, but when I suggested it might be too hot, he just looked at me like I was a real wimp. After the whirlpool, he pushed me into doing several stretching exercises, obviously missing the full impact of my wincing. When therapy was over, he very tightly repacked my wound so as to rough up the eschar when the packing was removed the next day. Actually, he decided the wound should be packed two or three times a day to speed up the debriding process. This guy was all heart. Instead of putting a big gauze bandage over the hole in my leg, he chose a small one. He also said to forget about the three elastic bandages and get a shoe on my foot.

"Let's get rid of all this stuff that makes you feel sick. Start putting weight on that foot and stand on it more. Keep doing your exercises and you won't need to keep your foot up so much during the day. We'll have you back to your regular routine in no time. You should be driving by next week!"

I was getting accustomed to the sympathy elicited by my crutches and elastic bandages. I was not as eager to begin driving as the rest of my family was to have me drive. The sloppy, oversized sweats were comfortable and I had a good excuse for looking so slovenly. And most of all, I was acquiring a taste for country music.

Someone asked me one time if I knew what happened when you played a country western song backwards. His wife comes back, the horse and dog don't die, he doesn't lose his job, he stops drinking and nobody cheats on anyone else.

I think my physical therapist was just trying to get me to play the song backwards. He wanted me to get off the saddle and rock and roll!

DO YOU BELIEVE IN MIRACLES?

This year I didn't feel like writing the same old jolly Christmas letter to my friends and relatives. I sent this story instead.

In a big office, atop a huge building, worked three very intelligent, successful and wise scientists. Every night for the last twelve months they had strategically placed themselves in front of the windows that made up the perimeter of their office. Using high-powered telescopes and the latest satellite equipment, the three scientists were able to see a 360 degree horizon and track the smallest of stars.

Their job was to find and identify the Christmas star which had been predicted by other learned scientists to appear in the winter sky of the northern hemisphere in the year of our Lord, one thousand, nine hundred, ninety-three. Many scientific journals were filled with articles supporting and refuting the predicted appearance of a star that would light up the entire northern hemisphere, causing night to appear as day.

On Christmas Eve there had been no sign of that wondrous star. No heavenly bodies had been observed singing and rejoicing in the sky. It did not look as though their miracle would appear.

About sixty miles from the metropolis where the scientists kept their vigil of the sky above them, a twelve year old boy watched his flock by night. He did not have to sit with his sheep atop a snow drift, but kept one ear open for the sound of donkeys braying, their signal that coyotes approached. The boy was grateful for the safety of his flock, but still mourned the death of his Holstein calf last Fall.

He remembered the day he bought the crippled calf at the auction and brought it home to nurse it back to health. He could feel the warm breath of the black and white bull calf against his hand as he bottle fed him four times a day. He remembered how the little calf had walked with hooves bent under him until he was allowed the time and space to exercise his weak legs.

How he wished the calf had not gotten the scours. "What bad luck," he thought, "to get an early frost that chilled the calf and filled his lungs with pneumonia."

He had worked hard to save it and found little comfort in the words of old ranchers, "Nearly all bottle calves die of scours or something. Bottle feeding any animal is not an easy thing to do."

The young boy had not known that, for he had already successfully bottle fed several calves: a Brahma bull, a Scottish Highland bull and a Charlais heifer.

Under the same dark sky, on the same plot of land, a fourteen year old girl ran through the snow to the stable. As she checked the sleeping occupants of each stall, she was reminded of the twelve Dalmatian puppies that were born in the hay box. Two had died at birth and two more were born deaf. But she found a good home for all ten puppies and made enough money to pay for her horses for the next year.

She walked to Sunshine's stall. Big tears rolled down her cheeks as she thought of the Appaloosa mare that had taught her how to ride, how to win and how to lose. She remembered how excited she had been when Sunshine was bred and the ecstasy she felt on Memorial Day when Sunshine gave birth to a healthy Buckskin filly.

"Why did Sunshine colic six times in three months and finally have to be put down?" she thought as she scratched the beautiful filly behind her ears.

From inside the house "Hark the Herald Angels" came out of the mouths of two naked cherubs. Bath water dripped from their bodies and the seven year old cherub showed no signs of fear that such a display would lead to colds and chills, ear aches or strep throat. He had a new set of tubes in both ears and a tonsillectomy to thank for that.

The other little angel of five, danced around

the fireplace, singing and clapping, oblivious to the lingering scars on his hands from a hot stove several years ago.

Mother and father sat at the table waiting for their children to gather round. Father looked tired and worn, still trying to recover from the burden of missing so much work to care for his wife. She caught his eye and gave him a look that only the two of them understood.

They both gave a long sigh, remembering the day she tipped the tractor and pinned her leg beneath its weight. The sigh became a prayer of thanksgiving for her life, her leg and the ability to walk again.

Suddenly the door burst open and the two tenders of the flocks entered the room. A great tumult broke out as they shed their cold and damp garments and all the children clad themselves in robes of terry and velour to join their parents at the table.

The father helped his youngest son carefully light the single candle placed strategically in the center of the table. Mother turned out the rest of the lights and took her place at the vigil.

"This is the Christmas Candle," father said. "It is not only a symbol of the miracle of that first Christmas, but the miracles we have witnessed throughout the year."

In their big office, atop the huge building, the three wise scientists poised their telescopes high into the sky. They were so diligent in their efforts to prove the miracle of the Christmas star that they were unaware of the bodies below them.

Right under their feet, the metropolis and surrounding towns and hamlets were giving off a magnificent glow that turned the night into day. As far as the naked eye could see, small flickering flames from individual Christmas Candles affirmed that one does not need a telescope or the proof of wise men to believe in miracles.

COMPARTMENT
SYNDROME

Compartment syndrome. The doctor was afraid I might get it. It occurs at the sight of great pressure; where the tractor meets the calf, for example. The crushing pressure causes blood vessels to break and bleed into the tissue, which in turn can cause the tissue to deteriorate if the blood is not allowed to drain from the body. In most cases a hole has to be surgically made at the site of the pressure to allow for drainage. In my case, the pressure from the tractor caused my calf to split open on its own, providing the perfect drain.

I've known a lot of people with compartment syndrome, but never knew what it was called. You've seen it too, I'm sure. We all know someone who is hurting inside, suffering from a broken heart or a bruised ego. They hold it in and let it swell until a cancer or ulcer forms in its place or a heart attack sounds the alarm. What is held inside can kill us.

I didn't give a second thought to having my doctor examine my leg. In fact, no one even asked me if I wanted to get medical attention. They just loaded me into the truck and asked which doctor I wanted to see.

It wasn't that easy when my marriage was

suffering. My husband and I were separated and considering a divorce before we ever stepped foot inside a counselor's office. We chose a very nice man--a colleague of my husband's. Had he chosen the medical profession, he would not have been a surgeon. He didn't like to hurt anyone and he most certainly was not going to dig around and make any holes in an already suffering relationship. He made us both feel we were justified in our feelings. He sympathized with our predicament, took our money and informed us that 90% of all couples who separate end up getting a divorce.

At the time, neither my husband or I knew that we suffered from compartment syndrome, but we are both stubborn and took his remarks as a challenge to find someone who might force a change. We had nothing to lose and everything to gain.

Another colleague recommended a psychiatrist. This man was not afraid of the surgical knife and most likely enjoyed a brief internship in exploratory surgery! He knew all about compartment syndrome. He could cut a hole and drain the blood to the point you were in need of a transfusion!

The new therapist confronted every issue and was not afraid to crush a few toes. He made us take a long, hard, painful look at our childhoods and adulthoods. Thanks to his aggressive emotional surgery, we were able to heal our severed relationship from the inside out.

Ten years later, our marriage is solid. This is not to say that when the weather changes we don't feel some discomfort from our old wounds, but 90% of the time we're one of those 10% success stories.

The hole in my leg has not become a statistic. It is not yet healed. The plastic surgeon and the physical therapist both swear things are coming along nicely. But it's so slow! Months ago the plastic surgeon told me he could graft over the hole in my calf, but he would have to make a much bigger hole to do so and the scar would be about the size of a grapefruit instead of the size of a quarter. He also warned me that if I chose grafting, the hole might never grow shut under the new skin and there could remain a concave center to the graft, the perfect breeding ground for infection.

The surgeon and I decided to just leave it. Be patient. Let it heal. Feel the burn and the itching. Pound it with water. Fill it with gauze. Deal with it faithfully and one of these days the hole will be gone and the whole ordeal will be over.

I believe it will happen. I've experienced it before. It's just a very slow process, this healing from the inside out.

I'M JUST A BIT OF
A KLUTZ

I'm one of those people who can't chew gum and walk at the same time. I guess I'm just not very coordinated. When I made the pompon team in high school it was a great accomplishment to have actually memorized the routine well enough to fool the judges. The only flaw in my little charade was that I had to continue to work hard all year to fool everyone at every game.

When my husband and I took ballroom dancing in college, he thought it was embarrassing and foolish and didn't want to do it. It was me, however, who could not remember the steps. (Come to think of it, maybe it was me, not the class that embarrassed him!)

At the physical therapist's office I was put on a step machine and had to walk up and down steps for minutes and miles. I couldn't get it right for the life of me. AND he had to reteach me how to walk. Heal down... then toe... and up.

I have always been self-conscious and embarrassed by my lack of coordination. I felt it was a character flaw. It made me less than a whole person. I believed my brain was missing an important link.

I've changed my mind.

Have you ever stopped to think of all the things that the grey matter between your ears can do? Have you ever added up all the things it does at the same time? This is what my brain was responsible for during my accident.

It told me I was in big trouble.

It told me I was in big trouble and sent the big PAIN message from my leg to my brain.

It told me I was in big trouble, sent the big PAIN message from my leg to my brain and kept me breathing.

It told me I was in big trouble, sent the big PAIN message from my leg to my brain, kept me breathing and kept me conscious.

It told me I was in big trouble, sent the big PAIN message from my leg to my brain, kept me breathing, kept me conscious and kept my bladder and bowels under control.

It told me I was in big trouble, sent

the big PAIN message from my leg
to my brain, kept me breathing, kept
me conscious, kept my bladder and
bowels   under   control,   and
remembered my hypnosis classes for
child birth, interpreting the tractor as
a possible fifth child and made me
count and breathe so I could tolerate
the pain.

It told me I was in big trouble, sent
the big PAIN message from my leg
to my brain, kept me breathing, kept
me conscious, kept my bladder and
bowels under control, remembered
my hypnosis classes so I could tolerate the pain and made my hand
push the horn on the tractor.

It told me I was in big trouble, sent
the big PAIN message from my leg
to my brain, kept me breathing, kept
me conscious, kept my bladder and
bowels under control, remembered
my hypnosis classes so I could tolerate the pain, made my hand push
the horn on the tractor and allowed
me to hear and respond to the

questions being asked of me.

It told me I was in big trouble, sent
the big PAIN message from my leg
to my brain, kept me breathing, kept
me conscious, kept my bladder and
bowels under control, remembered
my hypnosis classes so I could tolerate the pain, made my hand push
the horn on the tractor, allowed me to
hear and respond to the questions
being asked of me and reassured me
that I was not going to die.

Any brain that can do all that is not missing
any links, especially any important ones. The
human brain is magnificent. Mine served me well
when Missy fell on me. Not once did I have to tell
it to do any of those things. Like an airplane flying
on automatic pilot, my brain kept me going when I
was in shock.

If it takes me longer than most to learn the
Fox trot and my Jitter-bugging appears less than
cool, I can live with that. When it really counts, my
brain functions as smooth as a waltz on ice and I can
live with that!

106

MIRROR, MIRROR
ON THE WALL

I'm vain and somewhat embarrassed by it.
I used to pride myself on being 99 1/100% pure, just
like the soap. As a teenager in the late sixties and
early seventies, I was a hippie wanna-be. Natural
was in. So was telling it like it is and exposing
hypocrisy.

My hair was naturally curly when all the
other flower children's hair was long and straight.
When women were just beginning to let it all hang
out, I had nothing to support, let alone hang! At an
early age I found out that lack of vanity is a gift
given to a privileged few; women who are born
beautiful, selfless, and kind hearted with tiny, high
pitched voices. Like Snow White!

In my life, vanity has come and gone in
stages. In high school I sat under a drier for hours
with my long hair wrapped around orange cans to
straighten the curls. I wore saddle shoes and knee
socks, not because I thought they were attractive, but
because they were popular. A friend and I also tried
the newest thing: fake nails. When mine wouldn't
stay on, I threw them in the trash. My friend
refused to give up, though; she held hers on with
bandaids.

In college I cut off my hair for the short,

sophisticated look. After I got a teaching job, I joined the frosted hair club. I didn't feel I had abandoned my principles. It wasn't dishonest. Who could I possibly be deceiving? No one's hair actually grows that way!

At work, I prided myself on dressing stylish, if not a bit eccentric. My goal was to not look like a teacher, because my husband, the therapist, says you can spot teachers a mile away by the way they dress. For a time, I even resorted to fake nails again, figuring after fifteen years the glue must have improved. Not! Having to stop in the middle of a lesson to glue your nails on or walking around with one hand stuffed in your pocket certainly lacks professionalism. One time I stooped so low as to send a student to the clinic for a bandaid!

Several times during my teaching career I tried growing out my hair. Vanity always stopped me from doing what I really wanted to do, though. My hair looked awful and it took too much effort and time to look even slightly presentable, so I always gave up and cut it in a stylish bob.

When we moved to the country I thought I could really develop the natural look again. Short nails aren't stylish, but practical, in the barn. Long, curly hair is in now and living in the boonies gave me a chance to hide from sophistication and let my hair grow.

Things were going just fine until one day my husband pulled a grey hair out of my head. I blamed him and the kids for it and dismissed it as absurd. Thirty year old women do not turn grey! Not! Thirty year old women **do** get grey hairs. After several children their bodies even begin to sag and horror of all horrors, hair begins to grow on their faces. It's disgusting. It's humiliating. And much more embarrassing than being vain.

Exercise, tweezers and a good beautician can do wonders for your ego. I am vain and it makes me feel good. Most of the time. You have to be careful, though. Being vain is a little like playing with matches. Handled properly, it can assist at romantic candlelight dinners and build passionate fires. If you use a match in a volatile situation, however, you're asking for trouble.

Two months after my accident my own vanity blew up in my face. I was still tending my leg, being careful not to introduce any infection into the wound. I had been told to cover it with gauze pads and silk tape to avoid skin irritation often caused by adhesive strips. One day I had an important meeting to attend regarding this book. I wanted to give the impression of professionalism that baggy sweat pants cannot convey. For the first time in ten weeks I put on a dress and nylons. Of course the big gauze strip looked tacky so I brought a box of adhesive strips from home and asked the physical therapist to put one on after my whirlpool. Just this once!

He agreed, but much to my dismay I had grabbed the wrong box and had to cover my wound with a green bandage with turtles and swords all over it. Luckily I brought a pair of boots to wear which covered the green bandage quite nicely. It should be noted that the boots would have also covered a gauze patch and their high, narrow heels made my legs ache.

The meeting was a success, appearance-wise anyway. No one knew what horrors I concealed under suede. Neither did I. When I removed the turtle bandage the next morning, a slight rash had developed where the adhesive had stuck to my skin. Five days later the rash was bright red, surrounded the entire wound and had infected the wound itself. Whirlpools were out of the question, expensive cream was applied to the itching rash and I was back on antibiotics.

I didn't feel too bright or beautiful then. I felt stupid and I wanted to kick myself. The next time I stand in front of the mirror and ask who's the fairest, I'm going to remember the day I used the green bandage and it will remind me that life's not fair. I'm just not Snow White. And no one expects me to be!

SORRY MISSY

I never did like that tractor.

It was strictly an issue of money. We didn't have any, yet my husband insisted we needed this tractor to plow ourselves out of the driveway. I saw it as another one of his expensive toys.

In his defense, I must admit he tried several options before signing on the dotted line at the Massey-Ferguson distributor. He had tried driving his 4X4 pickup right through the drifts in the driveway and we shoveled him out several times in the frozen night! He asked our neighbor to come over and scrape the drive with the blade on the front of his 4X4. It took the neighbor two days to get out of his own driveway and by that time we had shoveled ours clear to the road, by hand! We purchased chains and a blade for our small red lawn tractor. (Has the government ever done a study on why most pieces of large equipment are red?) The snow was so deep we couldn't find the little lawn tractor for three weeks!

Finally, my husband gave his eloquent closing argument about how missing a day of work costs more money than three monthly payments on a tractor.

Sold! One powerful red machine, with a blade on the back and a bucket on the front, sat in the warm, dry garage in the pickup's place; the pickup relegated to the cold, snowy driveway. Yes, it gets us out of the driveway after every storm. And yes, it is another one of my husband's expensive toys!

We were on speaking terms, however, and I had actually developed a fondness for the massive piece of equipment. It all began one afternoon in the early spring. There was no snow left on the ground, just huge, muddy ruts in the road. The children and I were all dressed up and going into town to meet their father at the Museum of Natural History and then go out to dinner. This was a treat.

Halfway down the driveway my mini-van slid off the main rut and down into a bottomless puddle of mud. I sat there literally spinning my wheels. There was no way out. Luckily I had a pair of boots in the van. I changed shoes and carried the two younger boys inside. I brought out boots for the older kids and then went back inside to call my husband and cancel our plans.

"You can stay home or," he said matter of fact, "wrap the chain around your bumper and pull the van out with the tractor."

I had driven the tractor back and forth on the driveway before, but never had I done such a daring feat. Could I actually do such a thing! Isn't that why people join AAA? Is this actually something anyone can do? A mother can do that?

"No, I don't think I could do that," was my reply.

"Sure you can."

"I wouldn't know how to hook it up."

"I'll tell you. Take notes if you need to."

With a sense of fear and a spark of power, I changed my clothes and mounted the red tractor. I drove it over to my little van and wrapped the chain around the bumper in just the manner my husband described so as not to pull the bumper off the front of the van.

I took a deep breath, ground the gears into reverse and pulled that baby back onto the road in one try! What power! What control! I felt like a god!

For months afterwards I told the story of me and my trusty tractor companion. My husband and I joked about offering women empowerment classes on the tractor. I finally understood man's infatuation with machines.

I was on the tractor often after that; moving manure, tilling the garden, digging a grave for my son's ewe. We were very familiar with one another. The tractor was my friend and I completely forgot what an ugly beast she could be.

As I look back on that fateful day in October, I realize that I had become much too familiar with Missy. So familiar that I acted cocky. I thought I could do anything with her without repercussions. I was wrong.

No matter how much you love someone, you should never let them drive without their seat belt. No matter how much you think you know someone, you should never push them down a hill in the rabbit gear when they really want to go in the tortoise gear! No matter how much you trust someone, you can never knock them off balance, like driving with the bucket up, and expect them not to fall! And no matter how much you love someone, how well you think you know them, and no matter how much you trust them, you're gonna get hurt if you get too cocky and take advantage of the relationship.

I haven't gotten back on Missy since the accident. I thought I was going to have to once and I got sick to my stomach. I'm sure we'll be riding together again one of these days. But neither of us has apologized to the other yet and frankly, I'm not sure Missy ever will!

I'M NOT SCHIZOPHRENIC,
REALLY

Some people might think I'm schizophrenic.
My life appears to be full of inconsistencies. To the
casual observer, I seem to function in at least two
worlds. I collect priceless art; an original oil
painting (a gift from my grandparents) hangs above
my fireplace. Original creations in mixed mediums
adorn my walls and refrigerator, and fingerprints are
etched in the sliding glass doors. I like cowboy
boots and tight jeans, metallic dresses and spiked
heels. I enjoy singing in the shower with the
country and western station blaring, yet quietly
enjoying an evening at the ballet. I often buy
expensive organic fruits and vegetables, but wash
down a burger and fries with a caffeine-filled
carbonated beverage. I hold two advanced degrees
in education and act as a consultant for a large
school district in Colorado. I believe education is
the hope of the future. That's why I home school
my children. I very much believe in the lessons of
the Bible, The Prophet, Erma Bombeck, and Shirley
McClaine. I have the highest regard for Jesus,
Buddha, Confucius and Ghandi. Their spirits live
today because they spoke the same truth.

I am not mentally disturbed, nor do I suffer
from schizophrenia. I prefer to think of myself as

one who suffers from an eclectic personality. Some people would have me believe that my personality is wishy-washy and makes me indecisive. This is not true. Because my options are vast and not limited to one doctrine, decision making is time consuming. My decisions can't be made based on habit or a single dogma. Many voices and numerous options must be considered. My thinking processes are not clearly defined in black and white, but rather visible in an array of colors, patterns and tones.

An eclectic personality is not void of morals, ethics, or feelings. Quite the contrary--I believe in truth, goodness, beauty and love. These beliefs underlie all my decisions. The problem lies in who's truth I choose to believe, what goodness and beauty I value, and what kind of love I want to surround my life. The foundation is there, I just have an array of choices as to how I build the framework of my life.

With so much time to sit and think after my accident, I began to define my life and the beliefs that are its blueprint. Here is what I believe to be true today. (Remember that I am an eclectic personality. I can choose to remodel at any time.)

I believe there is life after death, again... and again... and again. I believe that heaven and hell exist on earth and the way I react to the situations life presents me determines whether I live in heaven or hell. I believe the only meaning in life is what I give it and the purpose of life is to perfect the reactions and attitudes we have regarding change. I believe that prayer is powerful, not in manipulating God, but in manipulating the way I react to God's will.

I believe there are lessons to be learned in each life. This time around my lesson had something to do with learning to live in the present and the little red tractor was the vehicle used to help me arrive at my present destination.

When I was under the tractor, screaming for help and overcome with pain, I did not reflect on how I got there and what I might have done to prevent it. That was the past and totally irrelevant. Nor did I worry about who would pick my first grader up from school and what we would have for dinner or how I would be able to get to work the next day if they called me. That was the future. The sky could fall by then and all my worrying would be moot. Pinned beneath the tractor, all I thought about was that instant.

"Get this off, now!"

"Stop the pain, now!"

"Get me to the doctor, now!"

"Let this be over, now!"

For the next five weeks, when I was unable to do anything but sit, it afforded me a lot of time to reflect on the past and all the mistakes I had made and speculate about the future and all the catastrophes it may bring. I recalled meditating prior to my accident. During those times I was able to float above my life and gaze over it as if it were an expansive landscape. I could see all the peaks and valleys in my life and it was hard to distinguish whether the valleys were the low points in my life or welcome rest periods. Were the peaks mountain-top experiences or monumental obstacles to overcome? All I knew was that the peaks and valleys stretched beyond my vision in the past and continued over the horizon in the future and I could see that I had and would survive them all.

I know I must concentrate on the present. Doing my best, now. Confronting issues, now. Enjoying what I have and who I am, now. Life in the present defines the contour of the land. The here and now decides whether the valleys are peaceful and nurturing or dark and barren. Today determines whether my mountains are immense and insur-mountable or lofty and soaring peaks.

Living in the present is a noble pursuit. It's like having an eclectic personality; other ways are easier. I still kick myself for things I've already done, sometimes decades ago. And I am ashamed to admit that I fret and worry over things that have not as yet happened. What happens if we can't pay that bill? How are my children going to feel about me when they're on their own? Who will I be in my next life?

Really, I'm not schizophrenic. I just have a lot of things on my mind. And one thing I'm sure of is that in my next life I'm going to be an avant-garde, eclectic artist of the mechanical. Let me explain.

I plan on dismembering large pieces of farm equipment, which by that time could be obsolete anyway, and using the parts to make large, welded sculptures for parks and recreation areas. All the sculptures will be painted red and a brass plaque mounted on the bucket will invite everyone to walk all over it, trample it, hang on it, beat on it and abuse the indestructible metal as they wish.

I am an eclectic personality, remember. I believe that even red tractors have their place. Just not on top of me!

THE ULTIMATE
PARANOIA

Have you ever felt paranoid? Have you ever walked down the street and glanced behind you to check out the footsteps following you? Have you ever worried that a loved one isn't going to ever walk in the door again because they're already thirty minutes late?

I understand that feelings of paranoia are actually quite normal for persons who have been in an accident. It's a reaction to their brush with death. I felt it and sometimes still do.

I've never been one to believe that the whole world is against me and I can't trust anyone, but I must admit I am extremely cautious about making new friends or helping strangers. My husband stops to help every stranded motorist he passes on the road. I drive on by with the excuse that I am a helpless woman and what if this person is not really in trouble.

I have been known to stay awake at night when my husband is out of town, worried that the furnace will blow up or the barn will catch on fire while he's gone. I find much comfort and support in his presence even though I am sure things would be worse if something like that happened and he were here.

My husband was not at home, nor was he in town on the day of my accident. After I was back home and everyone knew I was safe, he arrived home to give me comfort and sympathy. Had he been home that day, several things would have changed. First of all, I would not have been on the tractor. Quite often, I take on additional responsibilities and risks when he is not with me. Second, had I tipped the tractor when he was home, I am sure he would have seriously injured himself trying to pick it up off me. Then both of us would have been writing this book. Third, I would have been less stoic and more frantic, relying on him to take control rather than myself.

I am also paranoid when I am tired, hearing noises and interpreting every little glitch as an omen. For the most part, I am a functional paranoid. I have not seen a therapist for this disorder because it really does not effect my daily performance. I do not lock myself in the house, afraid to face the world. And only occasionally do I lose sleep because of it. After my accident, however, the disorder escalated.

One snowy evening my husband decided to search for our donkeys using the tractor. He had been on the red devil several times since my accident without incident, but that night I had a fit and begged him not to take her down to the gully in the dark with ice and snow on the ground. I was paranoid that something terrible might happen. (I still think it would have been a serious mistake.) Thank heavens he indulged my paranoia and took the truck instead.

On another evening at dusk, my eldest son wanted to take the three-wheeler out to the field and cover his seedling trees with straw before the temperature dropped below freezing. His two younger brothers begged to ride along with him. My paranoia said it was a bad idea. Everyone could crash and burn and I would not be able to get up and help them.

That night my fear of being controlled by fear won out. I allowed all three boys to race across the field in the dark on another red vehicle. I'm so glad I did.

From my throne on the couch by the window, I watched their every move. The oldest drove with the middle one sitting behind him. The youngest boy sat in the little red trailer they pulled behind them. Perched on top of the bales of straw, he used an imaginary whip to encourage his brothers to pull him faster. Yee-haas and giddy-ups could be heard clear back at the house. Every once in awhile the three-wheeler would stop abruptly to let a brother off. He would then run ahead while the others chased him around the tiny trees.

The boys were out in the cold wind for nearly an hour. When they came in the house there was laughter and camaraderie that is so often missing between siblings. Under my breath, I thanked God for that moment; for the ability to ignore my fears and let my children live. That was not the end of my paranoia, however. I am afraid it has reached its peak. The ultimate paranoia is the fear of God. And I must admit, His power frightens me to death! I am worried about what He may have in store for me next. Someone once told me that God only gives to us what we are able to handle. I thought about this and wondered if it was really such a good idea to be so brave during my episode with the tractor. Was it really such a good idea to come out of this with a smile on my face? If I could handle this, did it make sense that God would try to give me something much more difficult the next time?

I began to ponder prayer. Only a few weeks prior to my accident I had begun to meditate on a regular basis. I had been wanting to meditate for years, but something always kept me from getting started. This time everything clicked. I actually felt the power of meditation come over me and I experienced positive results.

The words I chose to use in my meditation were planted in my subconscious by a minister at the church we were attending. She frequently used the term "lift them up" when referring to those about whom we shared concerns. I immediately liked the phrase and when I said it to myself, I felt light and unencumbered.

So it was that I would repeat the words "lift me up above my problems" over and over to myself each morning. Sometimes I would meditate 30-40 minutes before I felt a sense of well-being or interpreted some event as a sign of my unencumbered soul. One sign was as simple as my not getting irritated and yelling at my children when they interrupted my sacred meditation time.

I began to make it through each day without worrying about when the next check might come or how I was going to pay the electric bill. I was more relaxed with my children and the days went much smoother. Shortly after I began meditating, I was offered a consulting job that I had been assured earlier in the year would be filled by another person.

Things were looking up.

Then the tractor from hell ran its pitch fork into my leg!

Within hours of the accident my mind was spinning. Was this an answer to my prayers? Had God literally lifted me up and out from under my problems that day? Did the tractor tip so I might really believe in the power of prayer? Did He save my leg and my life to prove to me, as Jesus said, that if He clothes the sparrow, will He not do the same for me? Was the tractor a lesson in mind over matter? A lesson in trusting the unknown?

I'm not sure what **THE** lesson was--there have been so many. Was this meant as a crash course? Life Lessons 101, maybe? I'm still baffled and completely in awe of the whole situation, yet I believe the tractor changed my life forever and for the better.

But I must admit, there is one last confession I need to make. I am not totally cured of my paranoia. I have not been able to bring myself to meditate since the accident. It's not that I don't believe in the power of prayer and meditation, I most certainly do. It's just that I don't quite know what to ask for and how to do the asking. I need to be very careful and precise in my wording, you know. It just might come true!